BEFORE I GO

PREPARING YOUR AFFAIRS
FOR YOUR HEIRS

WORKBOOK

ARIE J. KORVING

KORVING AND COMPANY, LLC
SUFFOLK, VIRGINIA

Korving & Company LLC
Financial Planning & Asset Management
1510 Breezeport Way, Suite 800
Suffolk, Virginia 23435
www.korvingco.com

ISBN 978-0-9838785-1-3

Cover and text design by John Reinhardt Book Design

Printed in the United States of America

This Workbook is designed for my family, friends and caregivers to give them guidance regarding my wishes on my health care should I become unable to make my own decisions and my funeral when that time comes.

The Workbook contains information about finances and important documents. I have tried to keep the information up to date by reviewing it regularly. I have done this not to exert control beyond my time, but to help those I leave behind and make the settlement of my estate easier.

To my family and friends, this is my gift to you.

Contents

CHAPTER 1

A Message to My Family

Write a Final Message to your Family.

_____

_____

_____

_____

_____

_____

_____

_____

_____

_____

_____

_____

_____

_____

CHAPTER 2

Final Illness

The Advance Medical Directive is designed to make your wishes known about the kind of health care you wish to receive if you are no longer capable of making an informed decision. The Virginia Hospital and Healthcare Association, for example, provides Virginia residents the VIRGINIA ADVANCE MEDICAL DIRECTIVE. You should check with your state's association.

The relevent parts are:

- Appointment of Agent—this is the person you appoint to make health care decisions on your behalf.
- Powers of the Agent—a list of the decisions that your agent is permitted to make for you. Note that in certain cases a medical professional may have to attest that you are capable of giving your agent these powers.
- Health Care Instructions—where you specify what kinds of treatment you wish to receive or withhold.
- The "Living Will"—instructions regarding end-of-life care.
- Anatomical Gifts—where you provide for the donation of organs or your entire body.

Regulations may change the acceptable forms from time to time so the following form may not be the most current version. Consult with experts or visit your state's Advance Medical Directive web site.

VIRGINIA ADVANCE MEDICAL DIRECTIVE

I, _____, intentionally and voluntarily make known my wishes in the event that I am incapable of making an informed decision, as follows:

I understand that my advance directive may include the selection of an agent in addition to setting forth my choices regarding health care. The term "*health care*" means: the furnishing of services to any individual for the purpose of preventing, alleviating, curing or healing human illness, injury or physical disability, including but not limited to medications; surgery; blood transfusions; chemotherapy; radiation therapy; admission to a hospital, nursing home, assisted living facility or other health care facility; psychiatric or other mental health treatment; and life-prolonging procedures and palliative care.

The phrase "*incapable of making an informed decision*" means: unable to understand the nature, extent and probable consequences of a proposed health care decision; unable to make a rational evaluation of the risks and benefits of a proposed health care decision as compared with the risks and benefits of alternatives to that decision; or unable to communicate such understanding in any way.

This advance directive shall not terminate in the event of my disability.

(YOU MAY INCLUDE IN THIS ADVANCE DIRECTIVE ANY OR ALL OF SECTIONS I THROUGH V BELOW.)

SECTION I: APPOINTMENT OF AGENT

(CROSS THROUGH SECTION I AND SECTION II BELOW IF YOU DO NOT WANT TO APPOINT AN AGENT TO MAKE HEALTH CARE DECISIONS FOR YOU.)

I hereby appoint the following as my primary agent to make health care decisions on my behalf as authorized in this document:

_____

NAME OF PRIMARY AGENT   TELEPHONE   FAX, IF ANY

_____

ADDRESS   E-MAIL, IF ANY

If the above-named primary agent is not reasonably available or is unable or unwilling to act as my agent, then I appoint the following as successor agent:

_____

NAME OF SUCCESSOR AGENT   TELEPHONE   FAX, IF ANY

_____

ADDRESS   E-MAIL, IF ANY

I hereby grant to my agent named above full power and authority to make health care decisions on my behalf as described below whenever I have been determined to be incapable of making an informed decision. My agent's authority is effective as long as I am incapable of making an informed decision.

In exercising the power to make health care decisions on my behalf, my agent shall follow my desires and preferences as stated in this document or as otherwise known to my agent. My agent shall be guided by my medical diagnosis and prognosis and any information provided by my physicians as to the intrusiveness, pain, risks and side effects associated with treatment or nontreatment. My agent shall not make any decision regarding my health care which he or she knows, or upon reasonable inquiry ought to know, is contrary to my religious beliefs or my basic values, whether expressed orally or in writing. If my agent cannot determine what health care choice I would have made on my own behalf, then my agent shall make a choice for me based upon what he or she believes to be in my best interests.

My agent shall not be liable for the costs of health care that he or she authorizes, based solely on that authorization.

SECTION II: POWERS OF MY AGENT

(CROSS THROUGH ANY POWERS IN THIS SECTION II THAT YOU DO NOT WANT TO GIVE YOUR AGENT AND ADD ANY POWERS OR INSTRUCTIONS THAT YOU DO WANT TO GIVE YOUR AGENT.)
The powers of my agent shall include the following:

A. To consent to or refuse or withdraw consent to any type of health care, treatment, surgical procedure, diagnostic procedure, medication and the use of mechanical or other procedures that affect any bodily function, including, but not limited to, artificial respiration, artificially administered nutrition and hydration, and cardiopulmonary resuscitation. This authorization specifically includes the power to consent to the administration of dosages of pain-relieving medication in excess of recommended dosages in an amount sufficient to relieve pain, even if such medication carries the risk of addiction or of inadvertently hastening my death. My agent's authority under this Subsection A shall be limited by any specific instructions I give in Section IV below regarding my health care if I have a terminal condition.

B. To request, receive and review any oral or written information regarding my physical or mental health, including, but not limited to, medical and hospital records and to consent to the disclosure of this information.

C. To employ and discharge my health care providers.

D. To authorize my admission to or discharge (including transfer to another facility) from any hospital, hospice, nursing home, assisted living facility or other medical care facility. If I have authorized admission to a health care facility for treatment of mental illness, that authority is stated in Subsections E and/or F below.

E. To authorize my admission to a health care facility for the treatment of mental illness for no more than 10 calendar days provided that I do not protest the admission and provided that a physician on the staff of or designated by the proposed admitting facility examines me and states in writing that I have a mental illness, that I am incapable of making an informed decision about my admission, and that I need treatment in the facility; and to authorize my discharge (including transfer to another facility) from the facility.

F. To authorize my admission to a health care facility for the treatment of mental illness for no more than 10 calendar days, even if I protest, if a physician on the staff of or designated by the proposed admitting facility examines me and states in writing that I have a mental illness, that I am incapable of making an informed decision about my admission, that I need treatment in the facility, and to authorize my discharge (including transfer to another facility) from the facility.

(If you give your agent the powers described in this Subsection F, your physician must complete the following attestation.)

Physician attestation: I am the physician or licensed clinical psychologist of the declarant of this advance directive. I hereby attest that I believe the declarant to be presently capable of making an informed decision and that the declarant understands the consequences of this provision of this advance directive.

_____

PHYSICIAN SIGNATURE   DATE

_____

PHYSICIAN NAME PRINTED

G. To authorize the following specific types of health care identified in this advance directive even if I protest. *(Specifically cross-reference any applicable sections of this advance directive.)*

_____

_____

(If you give your agent the powers described in this Subsection G, your physician must complete the following attestation.)

Physician attestation: I am the physician or licensed clinical psychologist of the declarant of this advance directive. I hereby attest that I believe the declarant to be presently capable of making an informed decision and that the declarant understands the consequences of this provision of this advance directive.

_____

PHYSICIAN SIGNATURE   DATE

_____

PHYSICIAN NAME PRINTED

H. To continue to serve as my agent even if I protest the agent's authority after I have been determined to be incapable of making an informed decision.
I. To authorize my participation in any health care study approved by an institutional review board or research review committee according to applicable federal or state law if the study offers the prospect of direct therapeutic benefit to me.
J. To authorize my participation in any health care study approved by an institutional review board or research review committee pursuant to applicable federal or state law that aims to increase scientific understanding of any condition that I may have or otherwise to promote human well-being, even though the study offers no prospect of direct benefit to me.

K. To make decisions regarding visitation during any time that I am admitted to any health care facility, consistent with the following directions:

_____

_____

L. To take any lawful actions that may be necessary to carry out these decisions, including the granting of releases of liability to medical providers.

(Add below any additional powers you give your agent, limits you impose on your agent or other information to guide your agent.)

I further instruct my agent as follows:

_____

_____

_____

SECTION III: HEALTH CARE INSTRUCTIONS

(CROSS THROUGH SUBSECTIONS A AND/OR B BELOW IF YOU DO NOT WANT TO GIVE ADDITIONAL SPECIFIC INSTRUCTIONS ABOUT YOUR HEALTH CARE.)

A. I specifically direct that I receive the following health care if it is medically appropriate under the circumstances as determined by my attending physician:

_____

_____

B. I specifically direct that the following health care not be provided to me under the following circumstances: *(You also may specify that certain health care not be provided under any circumstances.)*

_____

_____

SECTION IV: INSTRUCTIONS ABOUT END-OF-LIFE CARE ("LIVING WILL")

(CROSS THROUGH THIS SECTION IV IF YOU DO NOT WANT TO GIVE SPECIFIC INSTRUCTIONS ABOUT YOUR HEALTH CARE IF YOU HAVE A TERMINAL CONDITION.)

If at any time my attending physician should determine that I have a terminal condition where the application of life-prolonging procedures - including artificial respiration, cardiopulmonary resuscitation, artificially administered nutrition and artificially administered hydration - would serve only to artificially prolong the dying process, I direct that such procedures be withheld or withdrawn and that I be permitted to die naturally with only the administration of medication or the performance of any medical procedure deemed necessary to provide me with comfort care or to alleviate pain. If I am an organ, eye or tissue donor (see Section V below), I want this instruction applied in such a manner as to ensure the medical suitability of my organs, eyes and tissues for donation.

In the absence of my ability to give directions regarding the use of such life-prolonging procedures, it is my intention that this advance directive shall be honored by my family and physician as the final expression of my legal right to refuse health care and my acceptance of the consequences of such refusal.

(Cross through Subsections A and/or B below if you do not want to give additional instructions about care at the end of your life.)

A. OTHER DIRECTIONS ABOUT LIFE-PROLONGING PROCEDURES

(If you wish to provide your own directions about life-prolonging procedures, or if you wish to add to the directions you have given above, you may do so in this Subsection A. If you wish to give specific instructions regarding certain life-prolonging procedures, such as artificial respiration, cardiopulmonary resuscitation, artificially administered nutrition and artificially administered hydration, this is where you should write them. If you give specific instructions in this Subsection A, cross through any of the language above in this SECTION IV if your specific instructions that follow are different.)

I direct that:

_____

_____

_____

B. DIRECTIONS ABOUT CARE OTHER THAN LIFE-PROLONGING PROCEDURES

(You may give here any other instructions about your health care if you have a terminal condition aside from your instructions about life-prolonging procedures, which are addressed in Subsection A above.)

I direct that:

_____

_____

SECTION V: ANATOMICAL GIFTS

(YOU MAY USE THIS DOCUMENT TO RECORD YOUR DECISION TO DONATE YOUR ORGANS, EYES AND TISSUES OR YOUR WHOLE BODY AFTER YOUR DEATH. IF YOU DO NOT MAKE THIS DECISION HERE OR IN ANY OTHER DOCUMENT, YOUR AGENT CAN MAKE THE DECISION FOR YOU UNLESS YOU SPECIFICALLY PROHIBIT HIM/HER FROM DOING SO, WHICH YOU MAY DO IN THIS OR SOME OTHER DOCUMENT. CHECK ONE OF THE BOXES BELOW IF YOU WISH TO USE THIS SECTION TO MAKE YOUR DONATION DECISION.)

❑ I donate my organs, eyes and tissues for use in transplantation, therapy, research and education. I direct that all necessary measures be taken to ensure the medical suitability of my organs, eyes or tissues for donation. I understand that I may register my directions at the Department of Motor Vehicles or directly on the donor registry, www.DonateLifeVirginia.org, and that I may use the donor registry to amend or revoke my directions; OR

❑ I donate my whole body for research and education.

[Write here any specific instructions you wish to give about anatomical gifts.]

_____

_____

_____

*(You **must sign** below in the presence of two witnesses.)*

AFFIRMATION AND RIGHT TO REVOKE: By signing below, I state that I am emotionally and mentally capable of making this advance directive and that I understand the purpose and effect of this document. I understand that I may revoke all or any part of this document at any time (i) with a signed, dated writing; (ii) by physical cancellation or destruction of this advance directive by myself or by directing someone else to destroy it in my presence; or (iii) by my oral expression of intent to revoke.

_____

SIGNATURE OF DECLARANT   DATE

The declarant signed the foregoing advance directive in my presence.

_____

(WITNESS)   (WITNESS)

This form satisfies the requirements of Virginia's Health Care Decisions Act. If you have legal questions about this form or would like to develop a different form to meet your particular needs, you should talk with an attorney. It is your responsibility to provide a copy of your advance directive to your treating physician. You also should provide copies to your agent, close relatives and/or friends. For information on storing this advance directive in the free Virginia Advance Health Directive Registry, go to http//www. VirginiaRegistrv.

org. This form is provided by the Virginia Hospital & Healthcare Association as a service to its members and the public. (June 2012, www.vhha.com). Please refer to the appropriate web site of the state in which you legally reside.

FURTHER INFORMATION

Each state has laws regarding Advance Medical Directives and you should consult with a medical professional, an attorney or a health care facility to make sure that you are using the latest approved forms for your state.

If you would like to explore this matter further, another good resource is the **National Healthcare Decision Day** website: http://www.nhdd.org/

There you will find a link to the American Bar Association Advance Care Planning Toolkit which gives advice on the following topics:

- Choosing Power of Attorney
- Health and Financial Decisions
- Making Medical Decisions for Someone Else
- Legal Guide for the Seriously Ill
- Myths and Facts About Health Care Advance Directives
- Understanding the Four C's of Elder Law Ethics

You will also find links to a number of other useful Internet sites that provide Advance Directives that you can fill out on-line or by hand and suggestions for how you and your family can communicate with each other about their health care preferences.

- Aging With Dignity (Five Wishes)
  The Five Wishes document helps individuals express care options and preferences. The advance directive meets the legal requirements in most states and is available in 20 languages for a nominal fee. Order online or call 850.681.2010.
- Caring Connections
  Caring Connections offers free, state-specific advance directives for all 50 states and DC that meet the legal requirements for each state. Download individual copies for free or call 800.658.8898 to have a copy mailed to you.
- Center for Practical Bioethics
  Caring Conversations is a workbook to help individuals and families communicate with each other about their health care preferences and contains advance directive documents. These forms are valid in every state when notarized and signed by two witnesses. Download for free or call 800.344.3829 to order.
- Compassion and Choices
  Compassion & Choices offers an advance care planning tool kit and state-specific advance directive materials.
- Lifecare Advance Directives
  The Lifecare Advance Directive website offers free state-standard advance directives for all 50 states, the District of Columbia, and four major United States territories (American Samoa, Guam, Puerto Rico, and the Virgin Islands). Research validated comprehensive advance

directives, as well as completion guides, agent guides, and other important advance directive support documents are also available.

- MedicAlert Foundation
The MedicAlert Foundation offers emergency medical information and identification services including Do Not Resuscitate Medical IDs and option to store advance directives for all 50 states.
- National Resource Center on Psychiatric Advance Directives
National Resource Center on Psychiatric Advance Directives offers general and state-specific information on psychiatric advance directives.
- Project Grace
Project Grace offers a free Advance Care Planning Document that is legally valid in states that do not require forms to be notarized. Download for free, or call 877.99.GRACE to order a copy.
- The Will to Live Project
The Will to Live Project provides state specific forms for designating an agent and stating health care wishes.
- The Patients' Rights Council
The Patients' Rights Council offers a Durable Power of Attorney document (in either multistate or state-specific versions) that expressly defines and prohibits euthanasia.

This is not intended to be an exhaustive inventory of Advance Medical Directive information, but a guide for you to use in preparing your family for the day that it will be necessary to have your wishes carried out.

THE LOCATION OF MY ADVANCE DIRECTIVE

Having an Advance Directive and a Living Will does little good if it cannot be used because no one knows you have it. Let your family know where your Advance Directive is kept and how to access it and if you have registered it with the Living Will Registery.

My Advance Directive can be found in:

_____

_____

_____

_____

_____

_____

CHAPTER 3

The Funeral

TO MY FAMILY: THE FIRST THING TO DO WHEN SOMEONE DIES

When someone dies, the first thing to do is to notify the appropriate authorities. Most deaths occur in a hospital where staff and doctors know what to do about pronouncing death. The hospital staff will assist the family in contacting the funeral home.

If the death occurs at home, *dial 911* and an emergency response team will be dispatched to assist you. When the paramedics arrive, they will determine whether death has occurred and usually will be able to determine the cause of death. Once death has been established, the funeral home can be contacted. If the family is a member of or attends a church, the pastor can also be called to provide grief counseling and help with funeral arrangements.

If death occurs while on travel, call 911, and then call a funeral home in that area. They will prepare the body for shipment home and arrange for your local funeral home to receive the body.

MY PERSONAL INFORMATION NEEDED FOR THE FUNERAL PROCESS

The following information is required for important papers, such as the death certificate. Your family will need this basic information at a very stressful time. For record-keeping purposes, duplicate information forms are included for both spouses or partners. Please take time now to fill it out, and remember to review it at least once a year. A good habit to get into might be to review the information every January 1, or perhaps annually on your birthday.

Full legal name: _____

Street address: _____

City: _____

State/Zip: _____

Date of birth: _____

Place of birth: _____

Social Security number: _____

Citizenship: _____

Length of residency: _____

Occupation: _____

Employer: _____

Date retired: _____

Type of business: _____

Number of years employed: _____

Mother's maiden name: _____

Her place of birth: _____

Father's name: _____

His place of birth: _____

EDUCATION

High School: _____
                       NAME   CITY   STATE

College: _____
                       NAME   CITY   STATE

Graduate school: _____
                       NAME   CITY   STATE

Other schools: _____
                       NAME   CITY   STATE

MARITAL STATUS

_____ Married   Spouse's name _____

_____ Single   _____ Divorced   _____ Widowed

MILITARY INFORMATION

Dates of service: _____

Branch of service and rank: _____

Service number: _____

Wars/Conflicts served: _____

FOR A MILITARY FUNERAL

Name of contact at nearest facility: _____

Phone number of contact: _____

RELATIVES WHO SHOULD BE CONTACTED

Here is a basic list of relatives and friends to contact upon my death. You may wish to expand it.

Spouse: _____

Deceased: Y _____ N _____   Place and date of death: _____

Wedding date: _____

Location of marriage certificate: _____

CHILDREN:

Name: _____

Address: _____

City & State: _____ Zip: _____

Phone: _____

Name: _____

Address: _____

City & State: _____ Zip: _____

Phone: _____

Name: _____

Address: _____

City & State: _____ Zip: _____

Phone: _____

Name: _____

Address: _____

City & State: _____ Zip: _____

Phone: _____

BROTHERS AND SISTERS

Name: _____

Address: _____

City & State: _____ Zip: _____

Phone: _____

Name: _____

Address: _____

City & State: _____ Zip: _____

Phone: _____

Name: _____

Address: _____

City & State: _____ Zip: _____

Phone: _____

Name: _____

Address: _____

City & State: _____ Zip: _____

Phone: _____

Name: _____

Address: _____

City & State: _____ Zip: _____

Phone: _____

CLOSE FRIENDS WHO SHOULD BE NOTIFIED

Name: _____

Relationship: _____

Address: _____

City & State: _____ Zip: _____

Phone: _____

Name: _____

Relationship: _____

Address: _____

City & State: _____ Zip: _____

Phone: _____

Name: _____

Relationship: _____

Address: _____

City & State: _____ Zip: _____

Phone: _____

Name: _____

Relationship: _____

Address: _____

City & State: _____ Zip: _____

Phone: _____

Miscellaneous but Important Information

Describe the location of the following documents.

Birth certificates: _____

Children's birth certificates: _____

Marriage certificates: _____

Deeds and titles: _____

Mortgages and notes: _____

Automobile records/titles/registrations: _____

Income tax records: _____

Veterans discharge papers: _____

Safe combination: _____

Passport number: _____

Electronic passwords: *As electronic banking and investing becomes increasingly common, you will want to insure that your survivors will continue to have access to the family accounts. Since bank and brokerage records are password protected, list the accounts and passwords.*

Account: _____ Web address: _____

User name: _____ Password: _____

Account: _____ Web address: _____

User name: _____ Password: _____

Account: _____ Web address: _____

User name: _____ Password: _____

If you are married, it is not certain who will predecease the other. For that reason, you should note:

SPOUSE'S DATA

Full legal name: _____

Street address: _____

City: _____

State/Zip: _____

Date of birth: _____

Place of birth: _____

Social Security number: _____

Citizenship: _____

Length of residency: _____

Occupation: _____

Employer: _____

Date retired: _____

Type of business: _____

Number of years employed: _____

Mother's maiden name: _____

Her place of birth: _____

Father's name: _____

His place of birth: _____

SPOUSE'S DATA (CONT'D)

EDUCATION

High School: _____
             NAME   CITY   STATE

College: _____
          NAME   CITY   STATE

Graduate school: _____
                  NAME   CITY   STATE

Other schools: _____
                NAME   CITY   STATE

MARITAL STATUS

____ Married   Spouse's name _____

____ Single   ____ Divorced   ____ Widowed

MILITARY INFORMATION

Dates of service: _____

Branch of service and rank: _____

Service number: _____

Wars/Conflicts served: _____

FOR A MILITARY FUNERAL

Name of contact at nearest facility: _____

Phone number of contact: _____

RELATIVES WHO SHOULD BE CONTACTED

Here is a basic list of people to contact. You may wish to expand on it.

Spouse:_____

Deceased: Y _____ N _____.   Place and date of death: _____

Wedding date:_____

Location of marriage certificate:_____

CHILDREN

Name: _____

Address: _____

City & State: _____

Phone: _____

Name: _____

Address: _____

City & State: _____

Phone: _____

Name: _____

Address: _____

City & State: _____

Phone: _____

Name: _____

Address: _____

City & State: _____

Phone: _____

BROTHERS AND SISTERS

Name: _____

Address: _____

City & State: _____

Phone: _____

Name: _____

Address: _____

City & State: _____

Phone: _____

Name: _____

Address: _____

City & State: _____

Phone: _____

Name: _____

Address: _____

City & State: _____

Phone: _____

Name: _____

Address: _____

City & State: _____

Phone: _____

CLOSE FRIENDS WHO SHOULD BE NOTIFIED

Name: _____

Relationship: _____

Address: _____

City & State: _____

Phone: _____

Name: _____

Relationship: _____

Address: _____

City & State: _____

Phone: _____

Name: _____

Relationship: _____

Address: _____

City & State: _____

Phone: _____

Name: _____

Relationship: _____

Address: _____

City & State: _____

Phone: _____

MISCELLANEOUS BUT IMPORTANT INFORMATION

Describe the location of the following documents:

Birth certificates: _____

Children's birth certificates: _____

Marriage certificates: _____

Deeds and titles: _____

Mortgages and notes: _____

Automobile records/titles/registrations: _____

Income tax records: _____

Veterans discharge papers: _____

Safe combination: _____

Passport number: _____

Electronic passwords: *As electronic banking and investing becomes increasingly common, you will want to insure that your survivors will continue to have access to the family accounts. Since bank and brokerage records are password protected, list the accounts and passwords.*

Account: _____ Web address: _____

User name: _____ Password: _____

Account: _____ Web address: _____

User name: _____ Password: _____

Account: _____ Web address: _____

User name: _____ Password: _____

OTHER CONTACTS

Record any regularly scheduled appointments you may have with physicians, dentists or others. List these people here so that the family can contact them after the funeral. Then your loved ones will not have the moment of pain from a reminder call about an appointment or a message to discuss an overdue bill.

Physician: _____

Phone: _____

Dentist: _____

Phone: _____

Optomologist: _____

Phone: _____

Hair Stylist/Barber: _____

Phone: _____

Other: _____

Phone: _____

Other: _____

Phone: _____

Other: _____

Phone: _____

Other: _____

Phone: _____

MY MEMORIAL INSTRUCTIONS

Record instructions for your memorial here.

Funeral home: _____

Address: _____

Telephone: _____

I have _____ Prearranged my funeral _____ Pre-funded my funeral

Viewing/visitation: _____ Yes _____ No

_____ Open Casket _____ Closed Casket

Location of ceremony: _____ Funeral home _____ Graveside

_____ Church _____ Other _____

(If a church ceremony is desired, refer to chapter 4)

Type of ceremony: _____ Traditional _____ Graveside

_____ Cremation _____ Immediate burial

_____ Other _____

Special ceremony: _____ Lodge Rites _____ Military

_____ Fraternal _____ Other _____

Type of casket: _____ Wood _____ Metal

Type of vault: _____ Steel _____ Concrete

_____ Other _____

Pallbearers: _____ _____

_____ _____

_____ _____

Floral request: _____

Memorial contributions: _____

Music: _____

Clothing: ____ Mine   ____ Purchase new clothes

Jewelry: ____ Remove   ____ Leave it on

Newspaper notice: ____ Yes   ____ No

If preplanning is simply not possible for you—for emotional or other reasons—you can still help your family by providing them with guidance regarding the funeral home, cemetery and other arrangements you would like made for you.

Dear loved ones, here are a few things I'd like done or not done at my funeral:

_____

_____

_____

_____

_____

_____

_____

_____

_____

_____

_____

If you have any special requests regarding the disposition of your ashes, here is a good place to mention them.

Instructions about my ashes:

_____

_____

_____

_____

_____

_____

_____

_____

_____

_____

_____

_____

_____

In the space below, jot items you would like mentioned in your obituary or death notice.

Information to include in my obituary:

_____

_____

_____

_____

_____

_____

_____

_____

Record any special wishes for your memorial service.

My request for special music: _____

Favorite scriptures: _____

Favorite poem: _____

Special decorations: _____

I'd like this special person or group(s) to participate: _____

_____

_____

_____

_____

CHAPTER 4

Financial Accounting

To My Family: This section of the workbook contains information about my will, any trusts, estate taxes, insurance, safety deposit boxes, bank accounts, investment accounts, and retirement accounts or other corporate benefits.

MY WILL

Record the location and information about your will, attorney, and executor here.

_____

_____

_____

You will find a copy of my will in: _____

The attorney who prepared my will is:

Name: _____

Firm: _____

Address: _____

City: _____State: _____ Zip Code: _____

Telephone: (_____) _____

The Executor of my estate is: _____

Address: _____

Telephone: (_____) _____

Special instructions:

_____

_____

_____

MY TRUST

If you have prepared trust documents, record their location.

A copy of my trust can be found in:

_____

_____

The attorney who prepared my trust is:

Name: _____

Firm: _____

Address: _____

City & State: _____

Phone: _____

Special instructions or comments regarding my trust:

_____

_____

_____

_____

_____

My Insurance

Insurance company #1: _____

Address: _____

City: _____State: _____ Zip Code: _____

Telephone: (_____) _____

Agent's Name: _____

Agent's phone number: (_____) _____

Policy number: _____

Death benefit: $ _____

Owner: _____

Beneficiary: _____

Location of policy: _____

_____

_____

_____

_____

_____

_____

_____

_____

_____

Insurance company #2: _____

Address: _____

City: _____ State: _____ Zip Code: _____

Telephone: (_____) _____

Agent's Name: _____

Agent's phone number: (_____) _____

Policy number: _____

Death benefit: $ _____

Owner: _____

Beneficiary: _____

Location of policy: _____

_____

_____

_____

_____

_____

_____

_____

_____

_____

_____

_____

Insurance company #3: _____

Address: _____

City: _____State: _____ Zip Code: _____

Telephone: (_____) _____

Agent's Name:_____

Agent's phone number: (_____) _____

Policy number: _____

Death benefit: $ _____

Owner:_____

Beneficiary: _____

Location of policy: _____

Insurance company #4: _____

Address: _____

City: _____State: _____ Zip Code: _____

Telephone: (_____) _____

Agent's Name:_____

Agent's phone number: (_____) _____

Policy number: _____

Death benefit: $ _____

Owner:_____

Beneficiary: _____

Location of policy: _____

Record any advice for your survivor(s) as to how your life insurance should be managed.

_____

_____

_____

_____

_____

_____

_____

_____

_____

_____

_____

_____

_____

_____

MY SAFE DEPOSIT BOX

Location of my safe deposit box:

Bank name: _____

Address: _____

City: _____ State: _____ Zip Code: _____

Telephone: (_____) _____

Box number: _____

The key is located in: _____

Here is a list of items in the box:

_____

_____

_____

_____

_____

_____

_____

_____

_____

_____

_____

_____

MY BANK ACCOUNTS

Here is a list of the banks at which I have accounts.

Bank name: _____

Address: _____

City: _____ State: _____ Zip Code: _____

Telephone: (_____) _____

Type of account: _____

Account number and co-owner (if any) _____

Personal banker: _____

Comments:

_____

_____

_____

_____

_____

_____

My Bank Accounts (cont'd)

Bank name: _____

Address: _____

City: _____State: _____ Zip Code: _____

Telephone: (_____) _____

Type of account: _____

Account number and co-owner (if any) _____

Personal banker: _____

Comments:

_____

_____

_____

_____

_____

_____

MY LIST OF INVESTMENT ACCOUNTS

Firm name #1: _____

Address: _____

City: _____ State: _____ Zip Code: _____

Telephone: (_____) _____

Advisor: _____

Account title: _____

Account Number: _____ Retirement account (Y/N) _____

Owner: _____

Value: _____

Beneficiary: _____

Portfolio manager: _____

Investment objectives: _____

_____

_____

_____

_____

_____

My List of Investment Accounts (cont'd)

Firm name #2: _____

Address: _____

City: _____ State: _____ Zip Code: _____

Telephone: (_____) _____

Advisor: _____

Account title: _____

Account Number: _____ Retirement account (Y/N) _____

Owner: _____

Value: _____

Beneficiary: _____

Portfolio manager: _____

Investment objectives: _____

_____

_____

_____

_____

_____

Firm name #3: _____

Address: _____

City: _____ State: _____ Zip Code: _____

Telephone: (_____) _____

Advisor: _____

Account title: _____

Account Number: _____ Retirement account (Y/N) _____

Owner: _____

Value: _____

Beneficiary: _____

Portfolio manager: _____

Investment objectives: _____

_____

_____

_____

_____

_____

My List of Investment Accounts (Cont'd)

Firm name #4: _____

Address: _____

City: _____State: _____ Zip Code: _____

Telephone: (_____) _____

Advisor: _____

Account title: _____

Account Number: _____Retirement account (Y/N) _____

Owner: _____

Value: _____

Beneficiary: _____

Portfolio manager: _____

Investment objectives: _____

_____

_____

_____

_____

_____

_____

Firm name #5: _____

Address: _____

City: _____ State: _____ Zip Code: _____

Telephone: (_____) _____

Advisor: _____

Account title: _____

Account Number: _____ Retirement account (Y/N) _____

Owner: _____

Value: _____

Beneficiary: _____

Portfolio manager: _____

Investment objectives: _____

NOTE: If you have more than five accounts, list each account separately.

_____

_____

_____

_____

_____

My 401(k)/403(b) Plan

Plan Name: _____

Company Contact: _____
NAME   PHONE

Value: _____

Beneficiary: _____

Here is what I suggest you do with this asset after my death:

_____

_____

_____

_____

My Deferred Compensation Plan

Plan Name: _____

Company Contact: _____
NAME   PHONE

Value: _____

Beneficiary: _____

Here is what I suggest you do with this asset after my death:

_____

_____

_____

_____

MY STOCK OPTION PLAN

Plan Name: _____

Company Contact: _____
NAME   PHONE

Value: _____

Beneficiary: _____

Here is what I suggest you do with this asset after my death:

_____

_____

_____

_____

Other Investments

Other than my personal residence, I have these properties:

Property #1: _____

Address: _____

City: _____ State: _____ Zip Code: _____

Telephone: (_____) _____

Type of property: _____

Tentants: _____

Income: $ _____

Location of the lease and other documents:

_____

_____

_____

_____

Other Investments (cont'd)

Property #2: _____

Address: _____

City: _____ State: _____ Zip Code: _____

Telephone: (_____) _____

Type of property: _____

Tentants: _____

Income: $ _____

Location of the lease and other documents:

_____

_____

_____

_____

CHAPTER 5

Financial Management

To my family: This section covers how and by whom I'd like my assets managed.

Here's my advice about managing the family assets:

_____

_____

_____

_____

_____

_____

_____

_____

_____

_____

_____

_____

_____

CHAPTER 6

Balancing Income and Expenses

MY INCOME SOURCES

Pension Income #1: $ _____ per year/month _____

Company/Agency Name: _____

Address: _____

City: _____ State: _____ Zip Code: _____

Telephone: (_____) _____

Person to contact: _____

The survivor benefit is _____ % of my income.

Pension Income #2: $ _____ per year/month _____

Company/Agency Name: _____

Address: _____

City: _____ State: _____ Zip Code: _____

Telephone: (_____) _____

Person to Contact: _____

The survivor benefit is _____ % of my income.

Social Security Income: $ _____ per year / month _____

Social Security Administration

Address: _____

City: _____ State: _____ Zip Code: _____

Telephone: (_____) _____

OTHER INCOME:

_____

_____

_____

_____

_____

_____

_____

_____

_____

_____

_____

_____

_____

_____

_____

_____

_____

_____

MY SURVIVOR'S INCOME:

"GUARANTEED" INCOME:

Social Security: $ _____

Pension income #1: $ _____   Source: _____

Pension income #2: $ _____   Source: _____

Pension income #3: $ _____   Source: _____

Annuity #1: $ _____   Source: _____

Annuity #2: $ _____   Source: _____

Other Guaranteed: $ _____   Source: _____

SUBTOTAL GUARANTEED: $ _____

PORTFOLIO INCOME:

Interest income: $ _____   Source: _____

Dividend income: $ _____   Source: _____

Rental income: $ _____   Source: _____

Business income: $ _____   Source: _____

Other: $ _____   Source: _____

Other: $ _____   Source: _____

SUBTOTAL PORTFOLIO: $ _____

GRAND TOTAL: $ _____

EXPENSES AND BILLS

My Internet bill-paying website: _____

My online User ID: _____

My password: _____

The following bills are paid automatically via monthly withdrawals from the following accounts:

1. _____

2. _____

3. _____

4. _____

5. _____

6. _____

7. _____

8. _____

9. _____

10. _____

Household expenses are as follows:

Expense	Monthly amount	Annual amount	Payment method
Mortgage			
Food			
Clothing			
Electricity			
Gas			
Auto			
Auto Fuel			
Home Maintenance			
Lawn & Garden			
Insurance			
Taxes (Federal)			
Taxes (State & City)			
Taxes (Property)			
Rent			
Restaurant			
Travel			
Entertainment			
Telephone			
Cell Phone			
Medical Co-pays			
Prescriptions			
Subscriptions			
Other			
Other			
Other			
Other			
Other			
Other			
Other			

NOTES

NOTES

ABOUT THE AUTHOR

ARIE J. KORVING is Chairman and co-founder of Korving & Company, LLC. Korving & Company provides financial advice and services to individuals, families, businesses, and nonprofit organizations. As people are living longer, retirees' concerns about outliving their financial assets has intensified. Korving & Company specializes in helping people prepare for retirement, manage their finances during retirement, and plan their estate. With more than 50 years of combined experience, Mr. Korving and his team have found that their guidance is especially useful to those who become suddenly single through the death of a spouse or a divorce.

Prior to founding Korving & Company, Mr. Korving was First Vice President, Investments with UBS. He has held management positions with General Electric and earned a B.S. in Chemistry from Michigan Technological University. He has been a CERTIFIED FINANCIAL PLANNER™ practitioner since 1993.

He currently resides in Virginia with his wife of over 40 years. They have two children of which he's exceptionally proud, and a growing number of grandchildren.

In his spare time he is an avid reader, gardener, photographer, and traveler.